I come from Hiding, Siren
Chaos, and Hunger.
I come from a long line of
Nazis, Swastikas, Star of D
Shelters,
Marching with pioneers, Da   ᵧ, ᵤᵢᵧᵢᵢᵧ, ᵤpotlights,
Applause, Travelling.
Having babies.
Being a mum.
Remembering.
Remembering.
Where do I come from? I really don't know any more.
Does it matter?
I just am.
Dorit Oliver-Wolff

**The stories in this booklet are extracts from my
public speaking and my memoires – the story of how
I battled to survive against all odds to rise from
Holocaust survivor to internationally renowned
recording artist.**

For bookings and to order copies of this booklet:

Website: **www.doritoliverwolff.com**
Email: **doritoliverwolff@hotmail.co.uk**

My Little Christmas Tree

Kaleti Paja Udvar is Budapest's main railway station. In the winter of 1943 my mother and I often spent time there. It was sheltered, warmer than walking the streets and fairly anonymous, as people were coming and going all the time.

My Mother was dressed as a Red Cross Sister in white with a red cross on her head scarf. If stopped and questioned, I was a patient she was accompanying to the Children's Hospital. I usually had a bandage over my face, covering my nose, my Jewish looks. At that time we were homeless and had no permanent address. Only after dark could we go to a "Safe House", which changed from week to week, sometimes even daily. We travelled by bus, tram or train. Like so many other Jews under the Nazi government of Hungary, we had to keep moving.

I was seven but so small and thin I looked like a child of five. I suppose travelling with such a small child was, for my mother, a mixed blessing. It made her less conspicuous on the one hand but added weighty responsibility on the other. We never carried suitcases as this too was an obvious give away for people on the run.

It was Christmas Eve and everything was lit up. My Mother bought me a little bag of roast Chestnuts. This was cheap, nourishing and kept our ice cold hands warm. The railway station was abuzz with people in a hurry to get home to celebrate. Strange, with all the sparkle and excitement, my main feelings, that evening, were tension and fear.

Suddenly the sound of Police whistles ripped through the air. From every direction Nazi Soldiers appeared with Alsatians and cordoned off the whole area. They were stopping everyone and demanding identification.
No one could escape the trap. My mother instantly headed towards an old woman who was selling Christmas Trees. She picked the smallest tree and, gripping my hand so hard I thought it would break off, she headed hurriedly straight towards a big, fat, red faced soldier in the cordon. In perfect German she asked him whether he could check our papers first as she was in a hurry to light the Christmas tree for me, her little daughter, before she went on duty at the Hospital.

'Of course my dear Sister', he replied, 'do not bother about papers. We are not looking for decent people like you and this lovely daughter of yours. We are seeking out the Stinking Jews; Scheis Juden. Happy Christmas Sister and God bless you and the little one.' He gave me a big smile, patted me on the head and stepped aside. We were let through the deadly cordon which was a death trap for so many poor Jewish people.

We almost ran but could not, as this would have caused suspicion. We looked at each other. I could feel my heart beat in my throat. My Mother just gripped my hand even harder. I was only seven years old but I knew. This time, once more, we were saved. If only for a night! This time, we were saved by that tiny, prickly Christmas tree.

Now I am over Seventy years old and every Christmas I remember. Every year it is the same. The little Christmas tree which saved our lives.

This is what Christmas means to me.

Nit Racing: A unique board game

Whenever my mother went out to work she would tell me that she would be back for me soon. The time was never set but she always kept her promise and I knew that no matter what, she would always come back for me. To ask, 'when?' never occurred to me, I just knew she would always care for me.

I was drawing when the door was suddenly thrown open. I had not heard even a creak on the stairs otherwise I would have known to hide under the bed or inside the wardrobe, as I had done so many times before. I knew that above all else, I must not be found. This time was different, they came out of nowhere.

Framed in the doorway stood two men in grey uniform wearing polished, black knee high boots. Between them stood our kind landlady, the one who gave me sweets and told me what beautiful eyes I had. But today there were no sweets, no smiles.

She looked at me with hard, angry eyes. "This is the little Jewish girl who has been hiding in this room". No one mentioned my mum and I was certainly not going to tell them. If they didn't know about her they couldn't find her and hurt her.

I was allowed to put my coat on and was then taken to a car that was waiting on the street. They asked me where my parents were but apart from that no one spoke to me.

The journey was not very long; I don't remember having been in a car before, let alone one as plush as this one. I leant back into the soft seats and enjoyed the glamour of the ride in such a car.

We came to a stop outside a grey flat faced building which had many floors and many square, blind, unblinking windows. The two men flanked me as we went through the massive, thick, double height door and along a long shiny-floored corridor; turning left then right until eventually we came to a room where I was left in front of another grey uniformed man who sat behind a desk.

He asked me so many questions and I couldn't answer any of them because I simply did not know. I was eight years old but my naturally small frame and lack of food for years meant that I probably looked about four or five years old. By now I was very scared, how would my mother find me here? I was worried I would never see her again but I was also worried that I would be in trouble with her if she ever did find me. I must have done something wrong. Why else would the landlady have called the soldiers to take me away? I didn't know what I had done but it looked as if the punishment was going to be one I wouldn't forget.

The desk soldier escorted me up some stairs and opened a door at the end of a corridor that was identical to the one on the floor below. He left me in a big room that was full of people all sitting in little huddled groups on the floor. Here were mostly adults, some my mother's age and some much older. I looked around and only saw one other child; a boy. He had a hunchback and his arms were very long in proportion to his body. He had fair wavy hair, blue eyes and somewhat protruding front teeth. Apart from this boy I was the only child in a room of about fifty adults. They were all so nice to me, they all wanted to protect and help me.

That first night, one of the older ladies put her arms around me and huddled me up close to her. Apart from when the hunchback boy taught me to play chess, I spent most of my time with her and she held me tightly each night. I still remember how her arms felt. I wish I could remember her name.

I never learnt his name but I remember another game the hunchback boy taught me. To pass the time, we had nit races. The rules were simple: on a piece of paper we drew as many lines as there were players.

Next we all picked a nit out of our hair. Each champion nit would then be placed on the line that had its owner's initials at the end. Then the fun would start; each 'trainer' would shout encouragement to their nit to urge it on to cross the finishing line first. Each new game called for fresh nits, and there was no shortage. Every competitor had a thriving stable of racing nits at their fingertips.

This stands out in my mind as enormous fun, a welcome distraction from the fear of what was going to happen to me next. I remember hearing several of the grownups pleading with the soldiers that guarded us. They begged them to take me back and kept repeating that this was no place for such a small child. I had absolutely no idea where I was or what kind of a place this was. I knew I was afraid and I knew that my mother would come for me. She always came.

Each day, the guarding soldier would come and choose five to ten people to take away with him. Every day these few would be replaced with new scared people all with yellow stars sewn to their coats. Relatives and friends pleaded to stay together No one knew where they were taken or what would happen to them. No one ever came back. This was a sorting centre. A transit camp from where we were sent to other, more permanent concentration camps.

One evening, a man in light brown overalls, who kept looking all around him, nervously came over to me and started to talk to me very secretively. I know he was talking to me but he kept his eyes looking everywhere but at me and it was obviously important that no one saw him or heard him.

He spoke very slowly and quietly. "I have a message from your mother". My heart jumped. "Now listen and listen well, there must be no mistakes. You must do exactly what I tell you to do if you ever want to see your

mother again. You must be very brave and do exactly
what you are told". This was the plan.

"After supper, when the lights are put out, you must
pretend that you need to visit the toilet, you must not tell
anyone what I tell you to do, not even your friends. They
could get into big trouble"

His voice was full of fear and I had no doubt that if we
were found talking it would be very bad for both of us.

He went on, punctuating each new instruction with "do
you understand?" I tried not to look at him but nodded
each time he asked. "Turn left and walk towards the
toilet. Opposite the toilet there is a corridor with a door
on the right. This is the room where the coal is kept. The
door will be unlocked. You have to get in and hide
behind the heap of coal. It is dark and cold and you will
be all by yourself but you must wait. You must wait until
you hear three knocks on the door. This will be the time
when the dirty washing is collected. The laundry trolley
will stop in front of the door. You must climb into this
trolley and hide yourself in all the dirty linen. Do not
forget to close the door of the coal room behind you. Get
as low as you can in the basket. Don't talk. Don't move."
He paused and rubbed his forehead with his hand. "The
trolley will be pushed by someone who will take you to a
place where your mother will be waiting." I turned to
look at his face but he stared steadily ahead, he went on.
"Whenever the trolley stops you must be completely
still. The soldiers will poke their bayonets into the bag to
catch anyone hiding. If you get stabbed, don't cry out, be

brave. If they catch you, you will never see your mother again". Now at last he looked at me. "Good luck little girl", he stared deeply into my eyes. "Your mother told me you were a brave and clever little girl and you can do this".

I felt so happy and I did exactly as I was told. The lights were out, everyone was huddled up. There were no beds so people slept on the floor under woolen blankets, all lined up and squashed together like sardines in a tin.

 Being close to another body keeps you warm so in the day people tended to sit up in the same places where they lay down to sleep at night. Occasionally we were escorted outside by soldiers with guns and fixed bayonets into a bare yard where we walked round and round before being herded back to the room.

When I opened the coal door I was amazed to see the huge mountain of coal. I was completely dwarfed by it which was a good thing because it meant that I could climb over and hide behind. Should anyone open the door, I would be completely hidden. I clambered on, right at the back of the heap of coal I found a blanket which I wrapped around myself gratefully. It was frighteningly dark but as my eyes grew accustomed to blackness, every now and then I saw a tiny blink of comforting light come through the keyhole from the corridor beyond. My excitement faded and the hours passed and I started to wonder whether I had been forgotten. After all, I was only a little girl, why would they remember where I was? I resolved that if no one

came for me I would sneak out in the morning and
pretend that I had been playing hide and seek. Time
seemed to lose its shape. For all small children waiting
seems endless and so 'are we nearly there yet?' is the
mantra of the very young. In that storeroom at eight
years of age, time had no middle and no end, only a vast
beginning with no markers.

I was freezing cold, despite the blanket and I worried
that my teeth were chattering loudly enough for me to be
heard by the soldiers. Several times I heard heavy
footsteps approach the door then go past. What if the
knocks never came? I remember thinking that I may die
in that coal room. It is odd that the thought was not
particularly frightening to me. Death was no stranger to
any of us and I accepted the possibility without fear,
probably because at eight I could not have imagined that
it was final. I knew I might die because that's what
happened to people like us in my experience.

Rather than fear, the overwhelming feeling that I do
remember was the longing to see my mother again.

Three short knocks! At last! I climbed out of my hiding
place and opened the door to see the same man in the
brown overalls who had spoken to me. He made some
room amongst the washing for me then, once I was in he
covered me with the grey, oily and smelly clothes and
told me to make myself as small as I could.

The ride was very bumpy, as the wheels were so very
small. From time to time it stopped and I heard the man

exchanging jokes with the guards. When the trolley was pushed down a few stairs I thought it would break in two and that I would surely be discovered. The stench in the trolley was so strong that my eyes were watering, I know now that the smell was urine and worse but at the time I couldn't imagine how clothes could smell like this.

Suddenly I was flying as two men swung the trolley onto the back of a truck. The truck lurched and swerved and stopped and started for what felt like an eternity but finally it came to a stop and a new man pulled me out, patted me on the head and called me a little hero.

And there, just behind the man, was my mum. Just as she had promised, she always found me. She handed something to the driver and they hugged. He ruffled my hair again and then climbed back into his truck and drove away.

We never went back to the place where the evil landlady snitched on me. Now as an adult, older than she was, I wonder what could make a woman call for the arrest of a small girl and send her to certain death. What terrible lack was there in her heart or what bitter poison had robbed her of basic human kindness? How evil we humans can be.

Then I think of the woman who folded me in her arms at night in that awful place and I wonder at how, in such grim circumstances, we can also be so noble.
Now when I play chess with my grandchildren I remember how I learned to play chess and I wonder what

happened to the blond haired, blue eyed boy with the hunchback.

The Kindness and Courage of the Enemy

When the SS discovered that I had escaped from the sorting house in Budapest, they would be looking for me and they would be looking for my accomplices because it would be unlikely that an eight year old little girl could have planned and executed such an intricate escape on her own.

'We are going to Pecs,' my mother told me. 'I was there when I was a little girl. It is much smaller than Budapest. I remember it was very clean, but it was a very long time ago.'

We headed straight to the central railway station, not returning to the place where the evil woman lived. I did wonder what could have possessed this woman to be so bad, so cruel and so heartless, to want to have me killed just because I was Jewish. Mum told me it was time to start somewhere new. The Gestapo would not rest until they found us, and by now the Germans had occupied Hungary.

The train journey was long but it did not matter because we were together again. I had found my Mum, we had been united, and that was all that mattered to us. All the time that we were separated all I ever wanted was to be with my Mum again. I used to cry myself to sleep, and I would pray that I would see her again.

Pecs didn't mean anything to me, all I knew was what my mother had told me and that there would be far less bombing than we had experienced in Budapest.

My Mother had an address for which we were heading. She had many connections. She also had many small pieces of paper on which there were names. My mother told me as little as possible, the less I knew the better and as usual she made a game out of each situation to ease the severity of our circumstances. It would have been too dangerous to ask too many questions which my mother could not have answered. She was constantly afraid of being found out. As a child it is almost impossible to keep secrets, so the less I knew the safer we were. I was a very inquisitive child so the easiest and safest way was to create a world of make-believe rather than reveal the reality would have been unbearable.

My reading was not too good as I had only been to school occasionally because we never stayed long enough in one place for a school to accept me. As a consequence my mother taught me how to read and write.

It was nice in Pecs. We lived in a lovely little place of our own and clung to each other, afraid to let go and relive the pain of the separation we had endured. There did not seem to be as many bombs here by comparison to Budapest, which was constantly being bombed. We only occasionally heard some explosions.

My Mother seemed to know lots of people who she met and with whom she talked. She had quite a lively social life. She was working in a school, teaching German. We both felt safe and settled. My Mother even had time to read me bedside stories and bed time became my favourite time of the day.

Little did we know that all of the 6000 Jews who had lived in Pecs and in nearby villages had been rounded up and sent by train to Auschwitz?

However one early afternoon there was a loud, unexpected knock on the door. Both of us froze in fear. We could not think who it could be. My Mother opened the door, and there stood two very tall German soldiers, dressed in black uniforms, with long leather coats and black boots up to their knees. Even their caps were black! They both had rifles and in the corner of the collar of each jacket there were two very close initials: The letters 'SS'.

'You have to come with us immediately.' These were German speaking soldiers. First they searched everywhere, opened drawers and rummaged through them, opened cupboards, looked under the beds, aimlessly searching. I did know what it was they wanted to find.

We were ordered to walk in front, with the two SS soldiers behind us, pointing their rifles and bayonets at us. They kept on shouting, 'Schneller! Schneller!' Which means faster, faster. My short little legs could hardly keep up.

 My grey, ribbed, knee-high socks kept sliding down to my ankles as the elastic was too loose to keep them in place. I kept on hobbling on one foot and trying to pull the socks up. The soldiers would not let me slow down and let me adjust my socks.

People stopped on the streets, looking at us, wondering what was going on, but nobody dared to ask. You could see the fear and the pity in their eyes. This sort of thing must have been a daily occurrence. They must have been thinking, 'There but for the grace of God, go I'.

I noticed, on the way, my Mother had put some scrambled up pieces of paper into her mouth and chewed and swallowed them. This she did very secretly and made sure the soldiers did not notice. I too wanted to help and chew some papers. We had never played this game before. I was really disappointed that she played this all by herself. I also felt I should not draw attention to what Mummy was doing. I had never seen her eating paper before. She must have had a really good reason to do this.

We stopped at a building which was guarded by two soldiers. These ones had grey uniforms and each had a rifle hanging from a shoulder. As we got to the big arched door the two guards saluted and clicked their heels when they saw the SS soldiers. Then they opened the doors for us. We were led up a few stairs through a shiny polished corridor to a room where a grey uniformed soldier sat behind an enormous, wooden, carved desk. He stood as we entered. He seemed to have been waiting for us.

The two soldiers in black saluted the soldier in grey uniform. He had many medals on his chest and many thin black stripes on his epaulettes. The men in black yanked their right arm suddenly up in the air with their palms open, and in unison they shouted, 'Heil Hitler!' at the same time clicking their heels. The soldier in the grey uniform and the medals did not raise his arm to reciprocate; he never even gave them a glance. Dismissively, he gesticulated with his right hand to encourage them to leave.

This room was bright, with big, circular windows that had seats beneath them. A large door led to the next room. This door was ajar and I noticed that this door was not like any other I had ever seen. It had something that looked like a quilt stuck to the inside of the door. Why was this door padded? The soldier in the grey uniform told my Mother to enter the room. In the middle of that room there were two chairs and a spotlight shining down at one of them. He told my mother to sit down on the chair within the light. He then turned to me and told me also to sit, pointing to the window seats in this office. He spoke in a very quiet and clear voice.

I could see my mother in the other room, sitting motionless on the chair with the glaring spotlight shining straight into her face. Her expression told me she was very frightened. I had never seen her look like that before. I was very panic stricken. It was as if every drop of blood was draining out of my body. I just wanted to go and hug my Mum.

The man slowly walked to his desk and sat down. There was a big pile of papers in front of him. He was reading though the papers very intensely with a very serious look on his face.

I sat quietly for a while where I was told to sit. Then I don't know what possessed me but I left the window seat and walked up to the desk behind which the man with the soft voice was sitting. I stood there silently for a while. Then I heard a voice coming out of my mouth involuntarily. In perfect German, I asked: 'Have you any children?'

He did not move. He kept his eyes fixed on the papers he was reading, but he stopped turning the pages. He didn't answer. After a moment, very slowly, as if in slow motion, he raised his head and looked at me, looking straight into my eyes. He had the most beautiful pale blue eyes. He took his time before he answered.
'Yes I do, two little girls. They must be just about the same age as you.' He picked up and handed me the framed photograph of two little, blonde, smiling, girls.

'They must be twins and about the same age as me.' I handed him the picture back and told him how lucky he was to have two such pretty daughters. Then I looked him straight in the eyes and asked him, 'Are you going to hurt my Mummy? Please let her go, don't hurt her. I don't have anyone else, just my Mummy. Why are we here?' I was speaking fluently in German.

He turned his head away from me. He did not say anything. He did not move. We were both motionless. Surprisingly I did not feel afraid of this man at all. All of a sudden he slammed both fists on the desk, 'Scheisse. I cannot do this any longer!' He got up and went into the room where my Mother was sitting, on the chair, in the middle of the room. I now noticed even the walls were padded. With his right hand he beckoned her to come.

Then he took out his wallet, in which I could see some more pictures of his two daughters, He took out all the paper money it held. I had never seen so much money in all my life.

'Here, take this,' and he pushed the money into my Mother's hands. 'Don't go back to your home. Go straight to the railway station. Take the first train out of Pecs. It does not matter where it goes. Just take your little daughter, who by the way is your guardian angel and a very brave little girl.' With these words he stroked my hair and gave me a little smile. 'Don't look back. Don't pick up any of your belongings. Just go as you are.' Then he addressed my mother, 'Not all of us Germans agree with what is happening, and we are not all heartless bastards.'

We followed his instructions. He accompanied us out of the building to the front gate. On the way the soldiers saluted him, and had very surprised looks on their faces but did not dare to stop him. Luckily the railway station was almost straight across from the Gestapo headquarter buildings.

We did not have to wait long. We got onto the first train that was leaving Pecs. Strangely, the train took us back to Budapest.

Mother was very quiet and so was I. While it was not obvious to me what it had all been about, I was very afraid for my mother. This game had been different from our usual games. This game was one we had never played before, and I hoped we would never play it again. Our most popular game was hide-and-seek, which could be funny sometimes, but this game was too scary!

Mother told me that this man had risked his life to save ours. We never found out what had happened to this amazing, brave man. If it was not for the compassion of this German officer, my Mother would have been tortured or even killed. She might never have come out alive or undamaged from this padded room. I often think of and thank this German soldier who gave us our lives back. This experience taught me that not all Germans were bad.

Years later, whilst discussing this episode with my Mother, she said, she thought she had been picked up, not because we were Jewish but because they thought she was a communist spy!

The Little White Nun

Christmas 1944 in Budapest was bitterly cold. Mother and I were roaming the freezing streets of Buda, which is opposite Pest, separated by the Danube River.

In Hungary, even during the war when there was very little food and not much reason for joy or happiness, people would still celebrate Christmas. Of course, everybody was frightened, depressed and hungry. The people's clothes were shabby. They mirrored the people's hopeless grey faces. But it was still Christmas, and that meant there was a buzz in the air and a lot more hustle and bustle than usual as people tried hard to make their lives more festive.

That Christmas Eve we had nowhere to stay, but my mother had been given the address of a place that we were told was a safe house. The house belonged to a vicar who had five children. Full of hope we searched for the house. He could not possibly turn away a young woman with a seven year old girl, not on Christmas Eve.

We got on the last tram that crossed the bridge from Pest to Buda, and then we had to walk for a very long time before we found the address. We searched for the house in the dark but it was very difficult to find as there were no street lights.

At last, there it was! A long pebbled footpath led up to a big, wooden, carved front door. My mum lifted the thick iron door knocker and knocked firmly. The door opened, just barely ajar, and the vicar peered out at us. Through the opening I could see a ceiling high Christmas tree, shimmering with glitter and Christmas decorations. It was beautiful. I had never seen such a wonderful Christmas tree. Five little children about my age were singing, laughing and dancing around this magnificent vision. The smell of food hit my nose and I felt my eyes close and my mouth began to water. I don't remember ever having experienced such a tantalizing smell. This made me realise how hungry I really was.

I hoped that at any moment I would be dancing and playing with the children, and could share some of their food. The exquisite smells wafted through the front door towards us. The nice warm air inside the house floated over me and felt like an embrace, it was so different to the freezing air where the two of us were standing.

The vicar pulled the door towards him even tighter so it was nearly closed. Only one half of his body was visible, the other half was firmly tucked behind the big wooden carved door.

"Sorry", he growled in a very deep voice. "You must be mistaken. You have been given the wrong address. You cannot possibly come in. "

"But my little daughter is only eight years old. We have nowhere to go and it is freezing. We are hungry. At least let us go to your cellar. Just don't let us freeze, it is Christmas Eve.", my mother pleaded.

My mother begged him to have a bit of compassion. He was a man of the church and even had his dog collar on. He should have understood, after all he had five children of his own. He slammed the door into our faces.

Seldom did I see my mother cry but this time she was bitterly sobbing. Everything seemed so sad and hopeless. It was I who tried to cheer her up. I tried to convince her we still had each other, and that this was the most important thing. I repeated the same words that she used to say to me when situations seemed hopeless.

Our relationship was not only mother and daughter but also war comrades. Although I was only five years old when the war started I had to become an equal partner in our fight for survival, and I had to pull my weight.

Usually my mother had a contingency plan. If one plan did not work out she had another one up her sleeve. This time it was not so. It seemed the end of the road. We had nowhere to go. Perhaps she was more upset because it was a man of religion who had turned us away, or perhaps it was because it was Christmas Eve. This was beyond her comprehension, just unbelievable.

We walked aimlessly on the completely deserted streets. We did not know which direction would be the best to take. The ice and the snow were glistening on the road. We could see how our breath turned into steam as if we had been smoking. It was so bitterly cold that we could not feel any sensation in our toes or fingers. The air burned our cheeks. The tears on our faces turned into icicles. We had to walk very slowly and carefully to make sure we did not slip, as the road was thick black ice.

It seemed as if we had been walking forever when at last we stopped in front of a big house with arched iron gates. Above the big door there was a small bell that sounded very nice when my mother pulled the chain to which it was attached. She had to ring many times but nobody seemed to want to open the door.

"This looks like a nunnery." she said to me. She put her arm upon my shoulder and squeezed out a little smile. She nodded reassuringly. "It will be all right, you'll see", she said.

She rang the bell again. The building looked very dark and forbidding. Eventually, after a long wait, the big door opened with a squeak and a groan, and a very small figure in a nun's attire appeared. She looked very young. She wore clothes that were a different colour from any nun that I had seen before. Her clothes were all white, so was her head dress, all pure white. Only the rosary and the large cross that hung down from her belt were dark.

"We have nowhere to go my little daughter and I," my mother began, "it is Christmas Eve. We are cold and hungry. Please can you let us in?" My mother's voice sounded very sad; pleading and tired.

There was a long silence before the nun answered and when she did, her voice was soft. She told us the building was no longer a nunnery but had been turned into a military hospital. The entire lower floor had been turned into operating theatres for high ranking officers. The nuns were a nursing order and were looking after the injured soldiers.

She whispered, "You see it would be impossible to let you in. There is nowhere you could hide, but I cannot turn you away either." She put her hand in front of her mouth and looked very frightened. For a moment she was hesitant, and then she turned to my mother and asked her. "Would you mind if I hide you in the loft? That is the only place where no one ever goes."

"Just let us in." Mother said eagerly.

Luckily, everybody was occupied with the wounded soldiers. As we followed the little nun through the endless dark corridors in the distance we could hear singing: "Stille Nacht. Heilige Nacht."

The three of us walked through dark corridors, and climbed seemingly never-ending winding steps. Eventually, we came to a locked door at the end of a corridor at the very top of the building. The little Nun stopped and unlocked it. She had lots of keys on her enormous key ring. She must have been the official key-keeper.

The loft was huge. There were a few small, blacked-out windows in the roof, but some tiles were missing, so we could see the stars.

There was lots of discarded furniture and boxes scattered around. The little nun and my mother chose the corner where we would settle, and then she told us she would be back as soon as she could, and she left us. Suddenly it was very quiet, dark and cold. After a while the nun returned, bringing us blankets and pillows. The dark did not seem so fierce anymore. Our eyes got used to the surroundings and the missing roof tiles gave us light. The stars were flickering and somehow it gave a festive feeling.

Although it was freezing cold, it was a lot warmer than being out on the street. At least the wind was not blowing. Here we were sheltered and we had blankets.

The little nun left again and when she returned she brought us bread and chicken legs, hidden in her apron. She even brought us a few biscuits. Now this was a real feast. We were warm, had a good meal, and we huddled close together, my mum and I, ready to sleep. When the Nun left us again we felt heavy and warm and safe.

We were just about to fall asleep when suddenly the silence was broken and all hell was let loose. We heard the roaring sound of the bombers, growling and groaning, becoming louder and louder. The sirens were shrieking, and then one bomb after another pummelled the building. Everything shook and the sky roared.

Amazingly, the little nun reappeared. She was out of breath and must have been running up all those stairs. She knelt down next to us, putting her little arms around both of us. She was crying. Through her tears she managed to whisper, "I cannot possibly stay downstairs safely in the air raid shelter, knowing that the two of you are here in the loft, which is the most vulnerable part of the building. God forgive me."

She clasped her little hands together, clutching her rosary, and looked up towards the sky.

"God, help us?" She kept on repeating this as if she was waiting for an answer from up above, and tears were rolling down her cheeks.

All this time the bombs were pounding the building as if it was specially targeted. I feel sure now that it was. The little nun sobbed and told us that she couldn't live with her conscience knowing we were up here. She had come to move us to a safer place.

Each time a bomb hit the building it shook violently. The earth was trembling, the walls were shaking. Bright red flames were licking the walls. There were lots of sparks, like fireworks. The black smoke was blinding, our eyes were burning with searing, painful tears. Then, suddenly, there was dead silence. We could not hear anything for a while. We went completely deaf. Luckily, this did not last too long.

The entire time we were holding onto each other tightly, not wanting to let go of each other. Then we heard the sounds of fire engines, many of them had arrived. They must have surrounded the whole building. The bombs and explosions were relentless. The thick black smoke

was just like in Belgrade only three years ago, when the
war first started and we had escaped from a burning
house. This had the same noise, same smoke, same fire,
and same fear.

We hurried to the door that would lead us to the inner
corridor. As the little Nun opened it we saw there was
nothing beyond the door! No staircase, no corridor, no
building, just an enormous empty nothingness. The rest
of the building seemed to have disappeared, sliced off
like a piece of cheese. Only the three of us were standing
amidst the fire and clouds of smoke, as if we cut off
from the rest of the world, marooned on the only
remaining part of the collapsed building. There was no
way that we could get down. We returned to the loft. We
could hear the fire engines and the voices of the firemen.
It was not dark anymore, the flames lit up everything.

Most of the roof had disappeared too. Hoping to get the
attention of the firemen we all shouted and screamed,
"Help! Help!" but we were petrified that nobody would
hear us through the chaos. The little Nun used her white
apron like a flag of surrender, waving it through the roof.
Miraculously a long ladder poked up through a hole in
the floor and three firemen appeared, ready to carry each
of us down.

The ladder was very long, wobbly and scary. I did not
dare to open my eyes and look down, but when I did just
for a second my head started to spin and I wanted to be
sick. So I quickly shut my eyes as tight as I possibly

could and held on to my rescuer until I was safely on the ground.

There were hundreds of people there. Everybody seemed to be talking at the same time. People were running around in all directions. There were nuns, firemen, civilians, wounded soldiers, some on trolleys, others in wheelchairs, but the majority of the military patients had been buried under the rubble.

Only a handful of the injured soldiers had come out alive. The bomb must have hit the house diagonally. It had sliced the building in a most peculiar way. As if by some miracle the three of us were saved high up in the attic, just hanging there whilst the rest of the building was destroyed. The bomb must have hit the operating theatres and the surrounding rooms where the majority of the soldiers were situated. Hardly anyone came out alive. If it was not for the compassion of the little Nun coming to rescue us she could have been one of the victims in the 'safe' air-raid shelter. Coming to rescue us saved her life too.

Luckily for us there was utter chaos. Nobody had time to ask questions. The little nun gave us a big hug. My mother and I were invisible. We vanished as soon as we could. We just disappeared. We ran as fast and far as physically possible.

Looking back from a safe distance, most of the houses around the nunnery were razed to the ground. It was simply unrecognisable. My mother and I looked at each other and wondered what had happened to the mean vicar's house.

For us this was a truly lucky Christmas. We had escaped death yet again

My Double Life

Having a Turkish policeman knocking at our front door in Istanbul was unusual and surprising, especially in the early hours of the morning, but when he showed my mother the extradition papers for me, issued by the Turkish authorities, we had the shock of our lives. I was only fifteen years old at the time, but according to Turkish law I was required to have a passport of my own. This was news to us, because up until that moment I had been included in my mother's German passport, which she had obtained by marrying Werner, a German.

I didn't qualify for a German passport, and as I was forced to leave Turkey within twenty-four hours my mother persuaded the German Embassy in Istanbul to issue me with an official travelling document. This enabled me to travel to Germany, to Augsburg, to live with my step-father's parents.

Being stateless means you are a persona non-grata. You are not allowed to enter any country without a Visa, and without a passport you don't get a Visa. That means if you don't have a passport, you are stateless. You are not welcome or wanted anywhere. For me it meant I could not travel back to Turkey to finish my schooling, as I did not qualify for a passport. The only passport I could have obtained would have been from Yugoslavia, but having a passport from Yugoslavia was a disadvantage because nobody would want to give you a Visa if you had a passport from a communist state.

Having spent a year in Augsburg, Germany, my German had improved immensely. To make the most of my time I joined a famous ballet school. Time was pressing as I had already lost a year of my schooling, and it was very important for me to find a way of returning to Istanbul. Luckily, my mother hadn't lost her touch for outlandish ideas.

One day she arrived in Augsburg out of the blue, waving a contract from the theatre in Istanbul that authorized her to create a variety show for the new season. In no time at all she had put an advert in the local paper: 'Auditioning for Singers and Dancers'. The plan was for me to be a part of this show. I had to audition like all the rest of the dancers, and I got the job. I was then able to get an artist Visa, and that's how I became a part of the ballet. After daily rehearsals we were ready, and within four weeks I was on a train for Turkey. This gave me the opportunity to continue my education.

This is where my double life started.

At night I wore fishnet tights, stiletto heels, false eyelashes, and marabou feathers, singing and dancing under the spotlight. During the day I wore my grey uniform, with grey knee-high socks, a navy neck tie, and I wore my hair in plaits.

Whilst it was very exciting it was also extremely risky because if I had been discovered dancing at night by any of the staff from my French convent school I would have expelled instantly.

The big opening night had arrived. I sat in front of a big mirror in the communal dressing room in the theatre. This was a large dressing room which we all shared. Each little space had a chair, a dressing table, and a big mirror framed by light bulbs to give maximum lighting.

The other girls were busying themselves unpacking their enormous make-up kits, ready for putting their make-up on, but I just sat there, looking around me, feeling panic-stricken and realising that I did not possess a single item of make-up. I had never even worn lipstick before. I was nearly in tears, just sitting there. One of the girls noticed, came to me, and asked me what was wrong. I explained to her that I didn't know what to do. The girls around me laughed in a friendly way, surprised. Then one of the girls simply took over my face. In no time at all two or three of the girls were covering my face in all sorts of creams and colours. Rouge on my cheeks, eyelashes, eye shadows and lipstick.

When I opened my eyes to see what they had done to me I could not believe what I saw. I looked like somebody else. I looked glamorous, and nothing at all like I usually looked. Oh my! Was this really me? Even the other girls were speechless. My transformation was unbelievable! I seemed to have become a glamorous showgirl. I looked like a real grown up.

I learned that stage make-up is different from everyday make-up. I was a quick learner. The foundation was a thick cream made by 'Leichner'. Most of the stage make-up was manufactured by this firm.

Once all the paint came off it was disappointing. All that glamour was gone. The girls looked at me from their mirrors. This was truly a double life. My whole persona seemed to change once I took my make-up off. How amazing it is to be able to create a completely different image with a bit of make-up and some know-how. Looking at my reflection in the mirror I was back to being a school girl again.

The routine of my double life would abruptly change daily, from sunset to sunrise. One morning after a French lesson, the teacher, an attractive youngish man, stopped me in the corridor. He looked very sheepish as he secretively glanced left and right to ensure nobody could hear him talking to me. His voice was so quiet it was almost like a whisper.

'Excuse me,' he said, 'May I ask you something? Do you have an older sister? Only last night I went to see the new variety show in the theatre and in the new German ballet I saw the most beautiful young lady. She sang with the most beautiful voice and I just couldn't take my eyes off her. It was astonishing how much she resembled you. Is she your older sister?'

At that moment I wished that the ground would swallow me up. I felt my face burning, I must have been blushing. Deep down I was afraid that one day somebody would approach me and find out, but my French teacher was the last person in the world I would have expected to be the one.

In hindsight I wish I had said, 'No, I don't have a sister.' Unfortunately I heard the words coming out of my mouth, 'Yes, I do.' He seemed very pleased with this answer. His eyes were gleaming, and a cheeky little smile appeared on his handsome face.

He asked, 'Please, could you ask her if she could meet me? I would like to get to know her. She is so beautiful.'

'Yes, I will ask her.' I replied.

I had to hold myself back, to stop myself telling him, 'It's me! It's me, you fool! Yes, I would love to meet you!' But that would have meant the end of my schooling, and I don't think they would have kept him on either. So, using my better judgment I told him I would ask her and I walked away, feeling my knees turning to jelly and hoping he wouldn't notice my wobbly walk.

After school I went straight to rehearsals because I had to turn into the 'other' me, the dancer and singer. This was a true double life. It was a very strange time for me. I felt like a child in a woman's world, but at school I felt like a woman in a child's world.

Interview by Oscar *Eastbourne, 2013*

My nine year old grandson called to ask if he could interview me about my experiences during the Second World War for a school project.

"Hi Nan," his little clear voice said on the other end of the line, "What was your favourite meal during the war?"

After a short thought, I replied, "I did not have a choice. Any food was my favourite food."

"Yes Nan, but what was your favourite?"

"Any food, as long as I got some!"

"What did you eat?"

"Mostly bread, if we were lucky enough to find some".

"Bread and cheese?" he asked.

"No darling we had no cheese."

"Bread and butter?"

"No darling, just bread, sometimes we dunked it in a bit of oil. We also ate potatoes, or scraps."

"What are scraps?" He wanted to know.

"Scraps are what you pick out of rubbish bins behind hotels."

A change of subject with more enthusiasm in his voice, he asked, "what was the fashion like?"

"There was no fashion, as such. People made their own clothes; knitted scarves or woolly hats. We wore hand-me-downs."

"What are hand-me-downs?"

"Clothing, shoes, socks. Anything the Red Cross would give you that other people did not want any longer."

"Nan, what was your favourite TV program?"

"We had no TV."

"But Nanny, what did you do? You were only a little girl. You must have been very bored?"

"No darling, I have never been bored. I used to sing, draw, and make up stories but above all trying to stay alive."

The phone went very silent. I heard my little grandson breathing.

After a while he had no more questions. Then a little voice said, "Thank you Nan. I love you."

TESTIMONIALS
From a student:

Hi Miss,
I wanted to thank you for your help in giving me (and everyone else) the opportunity to meet someone as amazing as Dorit Oliver-Wolff. It was an incredibly moving experience, and I wanted to say thanks for making it possible.If you could, could you also pass on my thanks to her, and tell her that it makes me so happy to see others standing up against discrimination and injustice towards others and trying to inspire others to do the same. Please tell her that she is so brave and strong, and that I can't begin to express how much I admire her. She is quite possibly the most amazing human being I have ever (and may ever) meet. She literally moved me to tears (which I can honestly say is a very rare thing to happen). Wish her the best for me and if you could please thank her so much for coming, for sharing her experience with us, for letting me take a picture with her and for the hug! I won't ever forget her, this experience or what she taught me, and I can't thank her enough.
I also hope that you have a lovely weekend! :)

E.W

TESTIMONIALS
From other students:

- 'It really furthered my understanding of the atrocity of the Holocaust.'

- 'Opened our eyes to what is happening around us and what we can do to change the world'
- 'A touching and motivational experience'
- 'Inspiring that someone who went through something so devastating can still be so uplifting'
- 'Dorit Oliver-Wolff was a true inspiration to go through all that and still be able to be as jolly as she was'
- 'Great to see such positivity from such a horrific event'
- 'Learning to respect other people independent of their race or religion is one of the biggest lessons you can learn. Dorit made me realise how lucky I am'
- 'Incredible experience. It was a pleasure to hear Dorit speak, who is so inspirational and so uplifting and through her story and charisma she made us realise how lucky we are and we must live life to the full.'
- 'It was a memorable experience'
- 'Inspiring. She changes your outlook on life as a whole.'
- 'To hear first-hand from the viewpoint of a little girl was extremely evocative'
- 'You hear or read stories but being able to ask a survivor questions was a real privilege'
- 'Grateful for hearing a survivor's story, and she was willing to share, and open my eyes to what was before, very little understanding of the Holocaust'

For Bookings:
Website: www.doritoliverwolff.com
Email: doritoliverwolff@hotmail.co.uk

CPSIA information can be obtained at www.ICGtesting.com
Printed in the USA
LVOW07s1927180315

431082LV00030B/1150/P